MARY STUART

First published in Great Britain
in Merlins in 1996

Text © John Hunter / Richard Oram

John Hunter has asserted his rights under
the Copyright, Designs and Patents Act
1988 to be identified as the author of this
work.

HB ISBN 0 86241 641 8

PB ISBN 0 86241 656 6

Cataloguing-in-Publication Data
*A catalogue record for this title is
available upon request from the British
Library*

Typeset and designed by
Artisan Graphics, Edinburgh

Printed and bound by
Oriental Press, Dubai

CANONGATE BOOKS LTD
14 HIGH STREET EDINBURGH EH1 1TE

MARY STUART

John Hunter
In association with Dr Richard Oram

CANONGATE • MERLINS

The Chronology of Mary Stuart

	The life of Mary	Events in Scotland	The life of John Knox	
1540	1542 born			1540
	1543 crowned Queen	1544–50 Rough Wooing	1546–47 seige of St Andrews	
		1546 Wishart burned, Cardinal Beaton murdered	1547–48 galley oarsman	
	1548 travels to France		1549–53 travelling in England and on the Continent	
1550				1550
		1554 Mary of Guise appointed Regent of Scotland	1558 writes 'First Blast'	
	1558 Marries Dauphin		1559 return to Scotland	
	1559 Queen of France			
1560	1561 return to Scotland	1560 Protestant religion established in Scotland	1560 issues 'Book of Discipline'	1560
	1565 marries Darnley		1564 Marries Margaret Stewart	
	1566 murder of Riccio son James born	1567 Battle of Carberry James VI crowned		
	1567 death of Darnley, marries Bothwell,	1568 Battle of Langside		
1570	imprisonment and abdication		1572 dies	1570
		1572 James Douglas, Earl of Morton, appointed Regent		
	1568 onwards: imprisoned in English jails			
1580				1580
	1587 Executed			

Chapter One

Mary's Early Years

In the magnificent palace of Linlithgow, in a room overlooking the loch, Mary Stuart was born on 8 December 1542. Several miles away, at the palace of Falkland in Fife, her father, James V, only thirty years old, was dying. His spirit was broken by the rout of his army at the hands of the English and he was desperately worried that he had no son to succeed him. Scotland's past had shown only too well the troubles brought by a weak monarch or the succession of a child-ruler.

A writer of the time described how James received the news of his daughter's birth:

'The news came from Linlithgow for the King that the Queen had given birth to a child. Being asked whether it was a boy or a girl the messenger replied, "It is a fair daughter." The King answered, "Farewell, it cam wi' a lass and it will gang wi' a lass." He spoke little onwards and he turned his back on his lords, his face staring into the wall. In this way, he died.'

Linlithgow Palace

James feared that just as his family, the Stewarts, had gained the crown through a woman, Marjorie Bruce, daughter of the hero-king, Robert, so it would lose it through a woman, his infant daughter.

Before she was a year old, Mary was crowned Queen of Scots at Stirling. Once more, Scotland was plunged into instability as noble factions vied for control of government while the queen was a child. The first few years of Mary's life were full of dangers and difficulties.

Although she was only a year old, Mary's hand in marriage was already sought by many foreign rulers. At this time marriages were often arranged for children by their parents. Mary's great-uncle, Henry VIII of England, wanted her to marry his son, Edward. He hoped that this would unite peacefully the two kingdoms, and some Scottish nobles shared his opinion and arranged a treaty with King Henry which provided for the marriage. But opposition to an English marriage was also strong in Scotland, and the treaty's opponents succeeded in breaking it. Infuriated, Henry resorted to force and invaded Scotland to make good his claim, but Mary was taken beyond reach of his armies, finding refuge at Inchmahome Priory on an island in the Lake of Menteith. Because of the destruction caused by the invaders, this 'courtship' became known as the 'Rough Wooing'.

The young Edward VI

The Family Tree of Mary Stuart

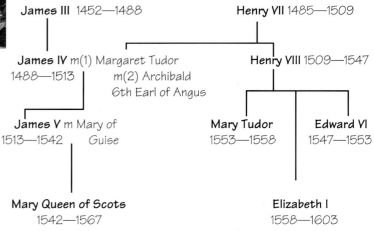

James III 1452—1488

Henry VII 1485—1509

James IV m(1) Margaret Tudor
1488—1513　　m(2) Archibald
　　　　　　　　6th Earl of Angus

Henry VIII 1509—1547

James V m Mary of
1513—1542　　Guise

Mary Tudor
1553—1558

Edward VI
1547—1553

Mary Queen of Scots
1542—1567

Elizabeth I
1558—1603

Soon afterwards, in August 1548, the five-year-old Queen, sailed from Dumbarton to France. She was accompanied by the 'Four Maries' – Mary Seton, Mary Beaton, Mary Fleming and Mary Livingston, who were to be her ladies-in-waiting – and they were to stay there for the next thirteen years. They sailed to north-west France by way of the west coast of Ireland to avoid the powerful English naval squadrons which patrolled the North Sea.

Study for a moment Mary's family tree. Her mother, Mary of Guise, was French, and it was hoped that Mary might reinforce the ancient ties which linked Scotland and France. The idea was that Mary would marry the heir of the King of France, the Dauphin Francis, thereby cementing another stone in the Auld Alliance – an agreement which had existed between Scotland and France for over two hundred years. The power of the English king was a threat to both Scotland and France, and so the two countries had made treaties to help each other if either were attacked by England. The alliance brought close contacts between the two nations, and many Scots had settled in France. French influence can be seen in the number of Scots words which have been adopted from the French language: for example, ashet from assiette, a plate or dish; fash from the verb fâcher, to anger.

Mary received her education in France, where she adopted the French form of the spelling of her family name, replacing Stewart with Stuart. She learned to speak French, Italian, Spanish and Latin; she was taught to sew, to write poetry and to play musical instruments; and she took a great interest in outside sports and pastimes such as riding and hunting in the French countryside around magnificent royal palaces.

A historian who had spoken to people who knew the young Mary wrote this about her: 'Her writing was clear and done quickly. Her excellence in singing arose from a natural, not acquired, ability to vary her voice. She played the harp and harpsichord. Being very agile she danced admirably... Several tapestries worked by her with wonderful skill can still be seen in France.'

To France

Mary of Guise

These were suitable accomplishments for the future wife of a king of France, but they taught her nothing about the skills needed for the government of her kingdom. She was in many ways ill-prepared for the troubles which lay in the future.

Her First Marriage

When she was only fifteen, Mary married Francis, who was a few months younger, in the magnificent Notre Dame cathedral in Paris on 24 April 1558. Francis adored his new bride. Here is how one of Mary's relatives described her:

'I think she will be a very beautiful girl, her complexion is fine and clear, the skin white, the lower part of the face very pretty, the eyes are small and rather deep set, the face rather long. She is graceful and not shy.'

The marriage ceremony was a splendid and glittering occasion. After the ceremony one historian recorded that: '... the heralds cried with loud voice three times "Gifts, Presents" and threw to the people great quantities of gold and silver ... and everyone pushed each other through greed to obtain some part of the money... Then there was a lavish, princely dinner prepared for the whole party; and after they dined they went to the royal ball. And as soon as the ball was ended they passed to the great hall of the royal palace where they ate a supper of such great magnificence that none of the servants there had ever seen the like.'

Mary and the Dauphin

Queen of France – briefly

Just over a year later, in July 1559, Mary's father-in-law died of wounds received in a joust, and she became Queen of both Scotland and France. She also, too, had claims to the English crown. Edward VI, the only son of Henry VIII of England, had died while only in his teens and had been succeeded by his elder sister, Mary Tudor. She died childless in November 1558, so Elizabeth, Henry's daughter by his second wife, had followed her on the throne. Although most Englishmen accepted Elizabeth, many Catholics believed that her parents had not been properly married and that Mary had a better right to the English throne. Because of this, the King of France laid claim to the English crown on Mary's behalf. Elizabeth never forgot that Mary, the Queen of Scots, had a claim on her throne and could be a threat to her.

Mary's happiness as Queen of France did not last long. Only two and a half years after the marriage Francis fell gravely ill. The ambassador from Venice saw little hope for his recovery: 'His life is despaired of. He still continues lingering without any hope other than in the mercy of God. The whole court is now constantly engaged in prayers.' Three days later, on 5 December 1560, Francis died. Mary was left a young widow, mourning the loss of her husband.

It was with understandable reluctance that Mary decided to return to her native country. Scotland meant little to her, because her life had been shaped in France. Judge for yourself her feelings expressed in the poem which she wrote on her voyage home:

Return to Scotland, 25 July 1561

> *Farewell my beautiful France, my dearest homeland,*
> *Who has cared for me during my childhood.*
> *Farewell France! Good-bye to happy days!*
> *The ship which is breaking up our love for each other*
> *Carries only half of me.*
> *As for the other part of me, it will remember you always*
> *Adieu, Adieu.*

The Scotland to which Mary was returning, however, was a vastly different place to the land which she had left twelve years before. After a long period of religious troubles, Scotland was in the process of changing from a Catholic to a Protestant country. This change lay at the root of many of the problems which Mary was to encounter over the following years.

Mary's return to Edinburgh

Chapter Two

Changes in the Church

The Catholic (or Universal) Church

This was a time of great change in Europe as well as in Scotland. Until the beginning of the sixteenth century the Catholic Church covered most of Europe, and the Pope, the head of the Church, was very powerful. To assist him to govern the Church, power was delegated to cardinals, archbishops and bishops throughout Europe, and a vast civil service in Rome helped his government to function relatively smoothly.

The Reformers

Since the beginning of the sixteenth century, some men in Europe had been trying to reform the Catholic Church. More and more people joined this movement for reform so that this period has become known as the Reformation. In Germany, a monk named Martin Luther (1483-1547) was one of the first to criticise the Church publicly. His ideas found wide support, and his followers became known as Lutherans. The arguments between reformers and Catholics in Germany became more bitter. Fighting broke out, and in 1529 the Lutherans protested against the actions of the Catholics. This protest was the origin of the word Protestant.

The reform movement spread across much of Europe, through Switzerland, the Netherlands, France and into England. The movement was slow to come to Scotland, though there were signs of discontent there. Some people in Scotland thought that all was not well with the Church, and decided that a large number of abuses and failings needed to be corrected.

Martin Luther

One criticism of the Church was that it was so wealthy, but made little use of its wealth to help the poor and needy. Each year, the Church's income from its land in Scotland was ten times more than the king received. Taxes, too, were paid to the Church, the most important of which were the teinds (or tithes) – a tenth part of income and produce. Other taxes were taken on special occasions, such as when someone died. The poet and playwright Sir David Lindsay wrote:

> 'Our Vicar took the best cow by the heid
> Within an hour, when my father was deid.
> And when the vicar heard tell how that my mother
> Was deid, frae hand frae me he took another.'

These taxes were usually paid in kind (the best cow, or a certain weight of corn) and not in money.

Another valuable source of Church income was the selling of indulgences to people who wanted to be let off the punishments which the Church imposed on them for the sins they had committed. Anyone could pay money to the Church, and in return they were given a document which stated that by paying the money they had done penance for their sins, and punishment had been cancelled. They could buy an indulgence for friends or relations, even if they were already dead. Some sinners came to believe that they could buy forgiveness while continuing to do wrong.

The wealth of the Church, however, was not enjoyed by all the clergy. The top churchmen were often very rich, especially when they controlled several churches at the same time, but many ordinary priests were extremely poor, sometimes little better off than their poorer parishioners. Vicars were poorest of all, and were so badly paid that well-educated men could not be attracted to the job, leaving it instead to men of inferior quality. Many vicars were ill-educated men, who knew little about the Bible, the Church or its teachings.

Some positions in the Church passed from one family

Failings in the Catholic Church

The selling of indulgences

Bishop Elphinstone

member to another. The Kings of Scotland did not try to put a stop to this, but instead put their own family and servants into key Church positions, often as rewards for loyal service or to provide for younger children. For example, James IV, Mary's grandfather, appointed his eleven-year-old son as Archbishop of St. Andrews, and James V persuaded the Pope to allow his sons, young and unsuitable though they were, to obtain good positions. To be fair, great care was taken over the education and religious training of the boy-archbishop, to prepare him for his position, and some royal servants appointed in this way, such as Bishop Elphinstone at Aberdeen, were deeply religious and hard-working men who took seriously the duties and responsibilities of their office.

Nobles also meddled in Church matters, and aimed to secure for themselves as much wealth and influence as they could. The people they appointed to important positions often cared little for religion or for ordinary Christians and frequently installed poorly-paid vicars to deputise for them and perform their duties in the parishes. As a result, many ordinary people were coming to have little confidence in their parish priest.

The Religious Orders

The picture presented by the other branch of the Church, the monks, nuns and friars, has often been seen as little better. Changing fashions had meant that few monasteries had been founded in Scotland after 1400, and monks in some older monasteries often lacked religious conviction or enthusiasm. Indeed, many monks and nuns were accused of using the wealth of their monasteries to pay for comfortable lifestyles rather than using it to allow them to work hard serving God.

Once again the picture was not entirely bleak, for not only were there still many men who unselfishly gave over their lives to the care of the poor and sick, and to devotion to God, but there were others who had sought – and succeeded – to instill new enthusiasm in their monasteries. Several Scottish abbeys were noted in the early sixteenth century for their spirituality and their monks were often highly educated. The Scottish friars too, after a long period in decline, had undergone thorough re-organisation and had largely returned to their original purity and simplicity. But this revival within the Church brought its own dangers, for some educated monks and friars began to question the Church's teachings and to criticise the wealth and luxury of their fellow clergy. A few were in touch with reformers on the Continent, and were sympathetic to their ideas. Indeed, some of the most fervent reformers were priests and monks who had become unhappy with their old way of life.

The picture opposite shows St. Peter, whom Roman Catholics saw as the first Pope, holding the keys to the kingdom of heaven. It symbolises how the Church was supposed to control entry to heaven. Anyone who opposed the Church could be excommunicated or expelled. People believed that this meant they would suffer everlasting punishment in hell. As you can imagine, this threat gave the Church tremendous powers.

Over the centuries, the Church formed many traditions which supposedly helped Christians lead good lives and reach heaven. An important place was given to Mary, mother of Jesus; statues of saints and rich ornaments adorned church buildings; relics of the saints were kept; confession of sins was heard and people were encouraged to do penance.

The reformers, however, thought traditions like these just got in the way of a Christian life. They did not agree that popes, or bishops and priests, controlled entry into heaven. In particular, they objected to the way the mass, a re-enactment of Jesus's last supper with his disciples, had, in their view, become distorted. They concluded that they must set up a renewed Church, free from influence from the pope. The reformers relied on the Bible, on ministers to guide people in their understanding of it, on simple services (a sermon, some hymns, psalms and prayers) and, above all, on each person's belief and faith in God and Jesus. Bishops had no place in such a Church.

The Power of the Church

St Peter holding the keys to heaven

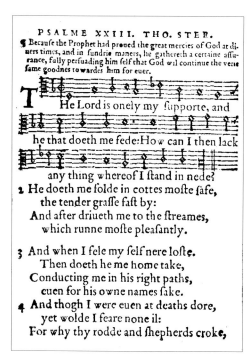

Psalm 23 from the 1565 Book of Common Order.

The reformers wanted ordinary people to be able to read the Bible in their own language. In the past it had been available only in Latin, a language only understood by well-educated people. Books were also expensive because they had to be copied by hand. The coming of the printing press from the Continent, first to England and then in 1507 to Scotland, meant that books became cheaper and more easily available. From the 1530s onwards printed copies of the Bible in English began to appear in Scotland, and from about 1560 the Book of Common Order was introduced for use in reformed Scottish churches. This was a service book produced for exiled English Protestants in Geneva which contained translations of the psalms and prayers in English, .

The Counter Reformation

While the reformers in Scotland were beginning to put across their ideas, the Counter Reformation in the Catholic Church was starting at the Council of Trent. This was an attempt by the Pope to reform the Church from within and so stop the spread of Protestantism. By the 1550s a new order of priests known as the Society of Jesus (the Jesuits), founded by Ignatius Loyola, was spreading across Europe with the intention of re-converting people to Catholicism. It was in the face of this movement for internal reform of the existing Church that the Protestant reformers in Scotland were to battle to build a wholly new Church.

Chapter Three

John Knox

Although there was no single leader of the Protestant movement in Scotland, one figure overshadows all his fellow reformers: John Knox. Knox became one of the most influential figures in the reformed Church, and it is largely through his writings that we know how the Reformation in Scotland came about, but we must always bear in mind that he presented a very one-sided view of events.

Early Life

While much is known about Mary's early life, very little is known about the early days of John Knox. Even the date of his birth is a matter of debate, although he is generally reckoned to have been born around 1512 to 1514 near Haddington in Lothian. Compared to Mary's childhood and youth, Knox's upbringing may have been quite peaceful, with little to disturb the prosperous burgh in which he grew up. He is believed to have been educated in the burgh's grammar school, where he received a firm grounding in reading, writing, mathematics and Latin grammar. From there he progressed to university, probably at St. Andrews, to study for the priesthood. He is believed to have become a priest before he was twenty-five.

His education may have sown the seeds of doubt in his mind, for he appears to have begun to question many of the central beliefs of the Catholic Church. By the early 1540s he was associated with the small group of men in Scotland who were convinced of the corruption of the Church and its need for reform. Despite Acts of Parliament designed to prevent the spread of Lutheran ideas in Scotland, calls for reform were growing.

John Knox

George Wishart preaching

The burning of George Wishart, from a book written in 1577

Alarmed by the demands for reform, the Church authorities attempted to clamp down on the more vocal reformers and a small number – about ten – were put to death (usually by burning at the stake). Such heavy-handed action, however, won sympathy for the persecuted reformers instead of turning public opinion against them. The picture on the left shows one of the early reformers, George Wishart, dying for his beliefs in March 1546. Wishart, who had lived in exile until 1543, may have been an agent in the pay of the English king, but was undoubtedly sincere in his Protestant beliefs. He was also one of Knox's personal friends, and his death had a deep effect on Knox, driving him still further from the Catholic Church.

In an act partly motivated by the desire to avenge Wishart's death, a group of Fife lairds gained entry to St. Andrews castle and murdered Cardinal Beaton, the Catholic Archbishop of St. Andrews and Chancellor of Scotland, who had ordered Wishart's death. The assassins garrisoned the castle and held out in the face of a siege by government soldiers, all the time expecting Henry VIII to send an English army to their aid.

Knox was overjoyed at the news of Beaton's death. He later wrote: 'How miserably lay David Beaton ... These are the works of God, whereby He would punish the tyrants of this earth'. Knox decided to commit himself totally to the reformers and he joined the assassins inside the castle in Spring 1547.

Since Mary was too young to rule for herself, the country was governed by a council led by the Earl of Arran, a weak and indecisive man. For various reasons – including the fact that his son was a hostage in the castle – he did not launch a full-scale assault. He feared that the English would aid the defenders, but did not wish to call on French assistance, for he hoped that his son would marry the Queen and suspected that the French would insist instead on her marriage to the Dauphin as payment for their help. To his fury, a French army arrived uninvited in Scotland, but their appearance brought a swift end to the siege. On 30 July 1547 Knox and his companions surrendered.

Overseas

Knox's punishment was harsh – he was sent to row in the French galleys. These were long warships propelled by huge oars, each oar needing several rowers to pull it. Rowing was back-breaking work, and the oarsmen were mainly criminals who had been sentenced to work in the galleys. Knox, like other prisoners, was chained to his oar and allowed little exercise, and was sustained on meagre rations while being expected to labour hard at rowing. Despite such conditions, Knox survived with his faith in the justice of his cause strengthened.

When he was released after eighteen months in the galleys, Knox travelled to England, Germany, France and Switzerland, the countries at the very heart of the Reformation. There he studied, preached sermons and formed his ideas for changing the Scotland he had so abruptly left. In particular, he visited Geneva where he met and talked with John Calvin, a leader of the Reformation on the Continent, whose ideas strongly influenced Knox's thoughts on religion.

Calvin, like Luther, had rejected the teachings of the Catholic Church. He believed that, although men were naturally wicked, God, in his mercy, had chosen a group of people who would be saved from eternal punishment in hell, but only if they stayed free from sin. He was certain that people who led wicked lives would be damned forever. Calvin had a much stricter outlook on life than Luther and he ruled over his adopted city, Geneva, with an iron hand, persecuting citizens whose life did not match his ideals.

John Calvin

His Return to Scotland

During Knox's years abroad discontent had grown slowly in Scotland and the ideas of the reformers had taken hold in only a few areas, mainly in the eastern burghs. The reformers lacked unity and national leadership, and in the early 1550s the Catholic Church believed that it had destroyed the Protestant movement in Scotland. In December 1557, however, a small group of Protestant lords, headed by the earls of Argyll, Glencairn and Morton, and the Angus laird John Erskine of Dun, drew up a document known as the First Band of the Lords of the Congregation of Christ. This was a manifesto which stated their intention to overthrow the Catholic Church and establish the Reformation in Scotland.

In 1558, the reformers felt that the tide was turning in their favour. In England, the death of the Catholic Mary Tudor had brought her half-sister, Elizabeth, to the throne. Scottish Protestants were encouraged that Elizabeth was a convinced Protestant and likely to favour change in Scotland, not least because it would see Catholic France's influence removed from Scotland. But the reformers needed to tread warily, and at first it was felt that Knox's fiery personality and outspokenness would do their cause more harm than good. An invitation for Knox to return in 1557 was withdrawn, but not before he had begun his journey. It was while he waited for fresh word from Scotland that he wrote *The First Blast of the Trumpet Against the Monstrous Regiment of Women*, a blistering attack on female rulers directed against Mary of Guise in Scotland and Mary Tudor in England. But the English queen had died and her successor, also a woman, was infuriated. It is easy to see why the Scottish Protestants, desperate for English aid, had doubts over the wisdom of calling Knox home.

The First Blast of the Trumpet Against the Monstrous Regiment of Women

The Reformation in Scotland

Despite their doubts, the reformers in Scotland knew that they needed the services of Knox, both as a preacher and as an inspiration to their cause. Decisive action was called for, as Mary of Guise, who had become Regent of Scotland on behalf of her daughter in 1554, was no longer prepared to tolerate the Protestants. In fact, she and her French allies seemed determined to stamp them out. In November 1558, letters from Scotland finally reached John Knox in Geneva, inviting him to return.

Before Knox arrived in Scotland in May 1559, the reformers took the offensive. In January, a notice known as the 'Beggars' Summons' was pinned to the doors of the friaries, calling on the friars to move out and let the poor have the buildings. In the coming months the friars, whose preaching was a threat to the reformers, bore the brunt of Protestant attacks.

On 11 May 1559, just days after his return, Knox preached a fiery sermon in St John's Kirk in Perth. A riot resulted, in which the church, one monastery and two friaries in the town were ransacked by his supporters. They believed that monasteries and friaries had no place in the true Church, and that rich ornaments were unnecessary. In the weeks which followed, wherever Knox and his fellows preached, monasteries and friaries were attacked, altars smashed and images destroyed. Parish churches, although stripped of Catholic ornaments, were generally not destroyed, because they could be used by the reformers.

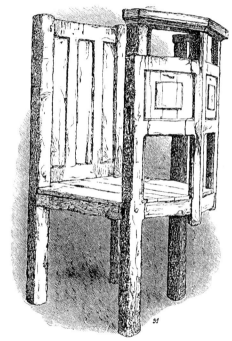

John Knox's pulpit in St Giles.

Knox's towering personality dominates writings about the course of the Reformation in Scotland, but at the time he was simply one of several leaders. Influential nobles, such as Glencairn and Argyll, or Queen Mary's half-brother Lord James Stewart, offered practical leadership in a struggle which had become a civil war. Mary of Guise had the support of few Scottish nobles, for even Catholics like the Earl of Huntly resented the way in which she had brought Frenchmen to aid her government. Her French troops were unable to defeat the Protestant lords, especially once Elizabeth of England sent soldiers to aid the reformers. It was only with the death of Mary of Guise in June 1560 that the war ended, and in a treaty drawn up the following month both French and English troops withdrew from Scotland.

Despite this success, the reformers were only a minority in the country. Their support came mainly from lesser landowners, from the merchants and leading men in the towns, and from a few of the greater nobles. Some of those who had sided with the reformers in the struggle genuinely did seek a purer religion, but others just wanted the Church's wealth for themselves.

The victorious Protestants, however, summoned a Parliament in August 1560, and with Knox's powerful encouragement behind them – but without Queen Mary's consent – it passed laws intended to change Scotland overnight from a Catholic to a Protestant country. These abolished the authority of the Pope in Scotland, and celebration of the mass, the main service of the Catholic Church, was forbidden and replaced by a new scheme of much plainer and simpler worship. It was, however, to be many years before these laws were made truly effective throughout the whole land.

Some of Knox's ideas can be found in his influential Book of Discipline (later known as The First Book of Discipline), seen as a blueprint for the new Church. Knox, for example, wanted congregations to

Edinburgh Castle, as is was in 1560 when the Scottish Parliament met there.

The ordination of Elders, painted by John Henry Lorimer

choose their own ministers. These ministers, with the help of elders and deacons (ordinary members of the church elected by their fellows), would maintain firm moral discipline in the parish. This was quite different from the old system, where congregations had no say in the choice of their parish priest.

Knox hoped that the reformed Church would not just concern itself with religious matters, but would also look after the poor and supervise schools. Parliament, however, thought that Knox's schemes were costly to run, and since it could not extract the wealth of the old Church from those into whose hands it had fallen in recent years, it rejected the Book of Discipline. It was some time before many of Knox's ideas were to be put into practice.

Although not all of his ideas had been accepted, Knox's views, and those of the Protestant lords, had been firmly stated. The question on everyone's lips was how the Catholic Mary would react to the upheaval on her return from France.

Chapter Four

Mary and the Reformers

Mary's Arrival in Edinburgh

Despite thick fog and rain, Mary, a young widow of eighteen, was welcomed enthusiastically by the crowd who turned out to greet her at Leith on 19 August 1561. Knox later wrote: 'In man's memory in that day of the year was never seen a more sad face of heaven that was at her arrival, which for two days after did so continue. For as well as surface damp and corruption of the air, the mist was so thick and dark that men could hardly see each other. The sun was not seen to shine for two days before, nor for two days after. This was God giving us some forewarning, but alas, the most part were blind to it'. Knox's hostility towards Mary is clear. We should be careful, however, in how we interpret his words.

This sketch of Mary's arrival at Leith in 1561 is taken from an old print.

THE ROYAL PALACE OF HOLY ROOD HOVSE.

*Holyrood Palace
around 1650*

Mary's new home was the Palace of Holyroodhouse on the outskirts of Edinburgh, outside the burgh walls. Inside the palace, Mary found some relief from the troubles of governing Scotland, and here she introduced the pleasures she had enjoyed in France – music, needlework, cards, dice, plays, dancing and splendid banquets. Outside in the parks around Arthur's Seat, she hunted, hawked, rode and played golf. Mary also kept a small number of French servants to remind her of her days in France. In their company she found the greatest pleasure.

Of great importance was Mary's decision to remain Catholic – she reached an agreement which allowed her, alone in Scotland, to celebrate mass in her private chapel. Yet, at the same time, she had no objections to accepting the Protestants' reforms. Mary was prepared to accept restrictions on what she did in public, provided she was allowed freedom in her private life. It was unheard of for monarchs in the sixteenth century to allow their subjects to hold views which differed from their own – especially as some Protestants believed that it was justifiable to overthrow a ruler who held what they regarded as wrong ideas.

It was inevitable that Mary and her beliefs would become the target of Knox's attacks. 'One mass', he declared, 'is more fearful than 10,000 armed enemies being landed in any part of the realm'. Nor was Knox the kind of man to dodge an issue. As one mourner later said at his grave, 'Here lies one who never feared the face of man'. Knox regarded himself as a crusading knight about to enter into battle with the devil; he feared that at the palace there was 'some enchantment whereby men are bewitched'.

Quarrels with Knox

Mary summoned Knox, her greatest critic, to Holyrood. On 4 September 1561 the first of several interviews took place. Although the discussions started civilly enough, the arguments soon grew heated. This battle of wits was felt by Knox to be of vital importance, since the future of Scotland could depend on the outcome. If he could overcome Mary's arguments and convince her that his ideas were correct, then the Reformation in Scotland would be secure. If, however, Mary remained unconvinced and a practising Catholic, the work of the reformers might yet be reversed.

The meeting between Mary and Knox, painted by Samuel Sidley in the nineteenth century

To make matters worse, Knox's writings which condemned women who involved themselves in politics and religion had angered Mary. She objected to his reference in the *First Blast of the Trumpet Against the Monstrous Regiment of Women* to females as 'frail, weak, feeble and impatient creatures'. She also protested against Knox's views that it was just for the subjects of an unworthy ruler who opposed God's rule to rise against them. Mary was not prepared to submit weakly, and as Knox remarked, 'If there be not in her a proud mind, a crafty wit and a stubborn heart against God and His truth, my judgement fails me'.

Knox, who had been appointed minister of St. Giles' Kirk in Edinburgh, continued to speak out against the Queen, and eighteen months later he was summoned again to Holyrood. This time Knox criticised Mary's lifestyle, especially her love of dancing which he detested. For her part, however, Mary regarded music and dancing as a pleasant way of passing the long dark Scottish winter nights, and saw it as a natural, graceful and artistic performance. Knox saw Mary's glittering court as offensive in the sight of God, and later claimed that Divine displeasure at her way of life saw famine inflicted on Scotland: 'In 1563 there was a universal famine in Scotland, but in the North where Mary had travelled before the harvest was taken in, the famine hit hardest and many died. The shortages of food were great all over, but especially in the North ... Thus did God punish the sins of our wicked Queen... The riotous festivity and huge banquets in the palace provoked God into this action'.

Musical instruments such as the virginal *(below) and the* stock and horn *(right) were used at Mary's court.*

Some of Mary's happiest times were spent hunting in the woods and parks of Falkland Palace in Fife.

Marriage Plans

Knox did not give up, and in a third confrontation he lectured Mary on the need to make a wise marriage, for re-marry she must. Mary was not an ordinary woman, she was Queen of Scots, and many European princes were anxious to win Scotland over to their side in their struggles for domination of Europe. Spain had remained Catholic; England under Elizabeth was Protestant, but France, the Netherlands and the Holy Roman Empire were divided. If Mary married a Spanish prince, she might overturn the Reformation in Scotland and throw her support behind the Catholics in Europe. If she married a Protestant, Scotland might help further the Protestant cause.

Despite his lectures, Knox had very little say in the issue of whom Mary should marry. Instead, her half-brother, Lord James Stewart, guided and advised her. He was especially anxious that Mary should marry a husband whom the English would find acceptable. This was because Elizabeth of England had never married and had no children, so it was possible that Mary, or her child, might one day rule England. As England was largely Protestant by this time, it was essential that Mary should marry a Protestant, for the English lords were unlikely to accept a Catholic ruler.

Chapter Five

The Royal Burgh of Edinburgh

Let us now look at Edinburgh, the royal burgh which lay at the heart of these events. By the sixteenth century it was the chief town of Scotland, yet it was similar in its layout and character to many other Scottish towns of this period. If we could visit sixteenth-century Edinburgh, we would probably notice immediately how small it was – a town of a few streets enclosed in a compact area with a population of about 9000. Today about 500,000 people live in the capital, which has expanded to cover huge areas which were farmland or open country in Mary's day.

Edinburgh, showing the Flodden Wall, from a map drawn in 1582.

A Fortified Town

To aid our imagination, we can consult this old map of Edinburgh. One of the most important features of the map is the long wall which surrounds the burgh. It was built to defend the town in 1513, when an invasion was feared following the crushing defeat of the Scots by the English at Flodden. The wall began on the south side of the castle and stretched round to the north, where the Nor Loch, which occupied the site of Princes Street Gardens, provided a natural defence.

Netherbow Port

There were several ports, or gateways, which were strongly defended, but were mainly intended to control the traffic of people to and from the countryside and into the burgh. For 250 years after it was erected, there was scarcely a house built outside the safety of the wall, because of lingering fears of enemy attacks.

The main fortification of the burgh was the castle. Like many other fortresses, Edinburgh Castle was built on a high point (part of an extinct volcano) which was easy to defend, and which gave a good view of the surrounding countryside. A small settlement had grown up around the castle as people sought its protection. Towering on its rocky crag and easily accessible only from its eastern side, the castle commanded a magnificent view over the surrounding area right down to the River Forth and across to Fife.

The High Street or Royal Mile

Running down from the castle was Edinburgh's main street, the High Street. Opening on either side were a series of closes (alleys) and wynds (lanes) where people lived crowded together. Immediately outside the castle was the Lawnmarket, the market place where people came to sell produce from open stalls. Later, separate markets were set up to sell particular products. They are remembered today in names like Fleshmarket and Fishmarket Closes.

St Giles

Walking down from the market you came to the ancient church of St. Giles. This was not the only church in the burgh, but as the parish church of Edinburgh it was the most important. During the Reformation it was cleared of altars, statues, images and everything linked with Catholicism. Here Knox was minister, and from its pulpit he preached his fiery sermons against Mary and the evils of the Catholic Church.

Partly hiding the church was the Tolbooth, where tolls or taxes on goods sold in the market were collected. It was also used as a jail and a court-house, and by both Scottish parliaments and the Edinburgh town council for meetings. A bell in its tower summoned the burgesses to meetings. It is recorded that the north gable was seldom without a human head stuck on it. It was the custom to display the heads of executed criminals in this way as grim warnings to wrong-doers. Outside stood rows of luckenbooths, or stalls, which sold a variety of goods. Unlike the Lawnmarket stalls, these booths were lucken, or closed, and thus could contain more valuable items.

Nearby stood the mercat or market cross, the centre of the town, where people assembled and where many public events took place. As the picture shows, the cross was an octagonal tower with eight turrets and a central pillar crowned by a unicorn. In front of it punishments were carried out: culprits suffered whipping, ear-nailing, branding, nose-pinching, tongue-boring and sometimes even death on 'the Maiden', a Scottish form of guillotine. In times of rejoicing, however, such as at a royal wedding, wine flowed freely at the cross.

Down the hill from the cross was the tron, a public weighing beam erected to cater for the expanding trade of Edinburgh. The weighing apparatus consisted of a pillar mounted on steps with a beam and scales attached.

What was life like in Edinburgh's High Street? Because everyone wanted to stay inside the walls for protection, land was scarce and houses had to be built higher and higher. It was not uncommon to see tenements constructed of wood and stone, up to fifteen storeys high; these were sky-scrapers of the sixteenth century. The crowded houses seemed even more densely packed because the tenants built wooden galleries and projecting staircases to reach other floors and buildings.

The result was a patchwork of houses closely knit together with no overall design. These areas were particularly dangerous in times of fire, since houses were crowded together, and there were few breaks to slow down the spread of the flames.

The Mercat Cross

This drawing of High School Wynd shows how close together the houses were.

The townspeople paid little attention to hygiene and sanitation. All kinds of garbage and litter were thrown out of windows into the streets with a warning shout of 'gardyloo' to the people below. The word gardyloo is from the French *garde a l'eau* meaning 'mind the water'! In the street, rubbish piled up in stinking middens and dung heaps which were only cleared periodically, and geese and pigs dug for food amongst the refuse. One of the first things you would have noticed in a sixteenth-century street was the overwhelming stench. Life inside tenements was little better. It was easy for disease to spread in conditions like this.

Since the High Street was so crowded, unsanitary and rowdy, the wealthier citizens moved into the Cowgate (the road leading to the pastures) where they founded an aristocratic suburb. People who lived in the Cowgate followed the latest styles in building, and many of the houses had fashionable timber fronts.

Another place where peace and space could be found was the Canongate, a separate burgh yet extending only down the hill from Edinburgh's east gate – the Netherbow Port – to the gates of Holyroodhouse. Here were to be found detached houses like Huntly House, still in use today as a museum. These new houses were often built of stone rather than timber.

In earlier times large forests had lain around Edinburgh, but by the sixteenth century there was a shortage of woodland to provide timber for building, and much had to be imported from Europe. It was this shortage of timber which largely caused folk to build instead in stone.

By the mid-sixteenth century, Edinburgh was Scotland's capital. It was here that Knox lived and preached. It was here, too, that Mary and her court spent much of their time after her return from France. It was inevitable in such a small community that there should be divisions over such an important issue as religious reform, and even as late as 1562 less than half the households in the burgh had committed themselves to the new Church.

Huntly House

Chapter Six

Mary's later Marriages

In 1562 Mary was still very much sought after as a wife. Suggested husbands came from all over Europe and included both the King of Sweden and the heir to the Spanish throne. The man who won her hand, however, was not a foreign prince but a Scottish noble, Henry Stewart, Lord Darnley, who from his birth in 1546 had been considered by some as a possible husband for Mary. As you can see from the family tree, he was Mary's cousin and also descended from the Tudor royal house, which gave him a claim to the English throne.

The prospects of an heir with strong claims to the English throne was not uppermost in Mary's mind when she married Darnley in 1565, but Elizabeth of England saw it as a further threat to her position and was infuriated by the marriage. She had not given her approval and Darnley, who had been living in England, had gone against Elizabeth's wishes. The marriage also ruined Lord James Stewart's careful work of smoothing the way for a future peaceful succession of a Scottish monarch to the English throne. Furthermore, Darnley

Marriage to Lord Darnley

Lord Darnley

James IV m(1) Margaret Tudor m(2) Archibald
of Scotland   6th Earl of Angus
1488—1513

James V m Mary of   Lady Margaret Douglas m Matthew
1513—1542   Guise   Earl of
                                                        Lennox

Mary Queen of Scots m Henry, Lord Darnley
1542—1567

James VI & I 1567—1625

was a Catholic, and many Protestants were alarmed by the prospect that his child, a future king or queen of Scots, would also be a Catholic and might seek to overturn the Reformation.

Mary cared little for what others thought of her marriage. New coins were struck to commemorate the occasion. She seemed to have found happiness with her new husband, but this did not last for long. Though he was described as 'the lustiest and best proportioned long [young?] man that she (Mary) had seen', Darnley was hardly perfect. Eighteen years old, he was vain, spoilt, weak, far from clever and preferred trivial amusements to the tedious business of government, yet he also bitterly resented the way in which Mary excluded him from the government of the kingdom.

Mary quickly recognised the mistake she had made. As she realised how shallow he was, her love for him faded. Increasingly, Mary went her own way and excluded Darnley from her plans. Darnley's feelings of being ignored and thwarted were increased by the attention which Mary showed to her secretary, David Riccio. An Italian of humble birth, his good looks, charm and musical talents appealed to the Queen, but his arrogance won him many enemies among the Scottish lords. He was also a Catholic, and the Protestant lords suspected that he was a papal agent. They resented his influence at court and disliked the idea of a Catholic dealing with the letters which Mary received from abroad, especially from the Pope.

Murder of Riccio

On the night of 9 March 1566 a group of conspirators aided by the jealous Darnley entered the palace. Let Mary herself, who was expecting her first child, describe the events which followed: 'We were in our room quietly having supper with a few friends and servants. Lord Ruthven, dressed in a warlike fashion, broke into our room with his followers and on seeing my secretary, David Riccio, amongst my servants, declared that he wished to speak to him... I said we would put David on trial before parliament to be punished if he had committed any offence. In spite of that, Ruthven advanced towards Riccio who had now gone behind my back and the table was knocked over... They then most

The murder of Riccio

cruelly took him out of the room and struck him fifty-six times with daggers and swords... We were also in fear of our own lives... All that night we were kept in captivity'. You can imagine the panic that gripped Mary.

Any love that Mary had for Darnley was now gone. Was it possible, Mary wondered, that the conspirators aimed also to kill her and her unborn child? For two days she was held prisoner in the palace, but she convinced Darnely that the other conspirators would betray him, and with his help she escaped by night and rode to Dunbar Castle. Her supporters swiftly gathered, and nine days after Riccio's murder Mary (with Darnley) returned to Edinburgh at the head of an army. The conspirators fled, and Knox, who had publicly rejoiced at Riccio's death, quietly left Edinburgh.

Birth of an Heir

It was into this turbulent world that Mary's child James, the future king of both Scotland and England, was born on 19 June 1566 in Edinburgh Castle. There was great rejoicing and 500 bonfires were lit. The Queen's new secretary described the scene like this: 'Immediately upon the birth of the prince, all the guns of the castle were fired, and the Lords, the Nobles, and the people gathered in St. Giles' church to thank God for the honour of having an heir to their kingdom'.

The Royal Chapel of Stirling Castle

On 17 December 1566, the young prince was baptised according to the rites of the Catholic Church in the royal chapel at Stirling Castle. Darnley, who was also in the castle, did not attend the ceremony.

Although she did not realise it, Mary was entering one of the most difficult times of her life. With her marriage in ruins and with groups of nobles openly challenging her authority, Mary felt in a desperate and weakened state. For support – and later for love – Mary turned to James Hepburn, earl of Bothwell, a man distrusted by Catholics and Protestants alike. A writer called George Buchanan claimed that she was infatuated with Bothwell, and that when news was brought to her at Jedburgh in October 1566 that he had been wounded and was desperately ill at Hermitage Castle, she immediately abandoned her duties and rode madly across the moors to comfort him. Buchanan was deeply hostile to Mary and always eager to discredit her, however, and his story is not supported by the official records. Mary's visit, which was made several days after news of Bothwell's illness was brought to her, appears to have been simply that of a monarch concerned for the health of an important subject.

Death of Darnley

Whether Buchanan's story is true or not, we do know that Mary no longer loved Darnley. What happened in the period after her visit to Hermitage is difficult to untangle. What is certain is that in January 1567, while he was staying in Glasgow, Darnley fell ill. Mary arranged for him to brought back to a house on the outskirts of Edinburgh at Kirk o' Field. It was a high, open position, in a far healthier site than Holyrood.

What then happened is far from clear. This is Mary's version of events: 'This is a horrible story. Last night, 9 February 1567, at two in the morning, the house in which the King (Darnley) was sleeping was, in a flash, blown into the air with such force that the whole house was demolished. Gunpowder must have been responsible but who is to blame I have no idea. Whoever it was will be harshly punished as a warning to others'.

Knox took a much calmer view of what occurred. He wrote: 'The surgeons, being convened at the Queen's command to view and consider the manner of his death, stated that he was blown up in the air and truly he was strangled. Soon after he was carried to the abbey and buried there'.

One thing that puzzled many people was that Darnley's body was found some way from the house. He appeared to have been strangled rather than killed by the blast, as Knox noted. The sketch below, drawn at the time, shows Darnley's lodgings reduced to rubble.

The question which has always divided historians is the extent to which Mary was guilty of his murder. Had she not brought Darnley to Kirk o' Field? Did she not despise him? Did she not plan to marry someone else? Rumours began to fly. The discovery later of the famous Casket Letters has added to the myths. These were supposedly written by Mary to Bothwell revealing her hatred of Darnley and her plans to have him killed. Mary strongly denied ever having written them. 'I have never written anything concerning that matter to any creature', she later stated. 'There are many in Scotland, both men and women, that can forge my handwriting'. Many experts do, in fact, believe that they were forgeries, but doubts still linger over Mary's actions and intentions.

*The sketch of
Kirk o' Field*

Of Bothwell's guilt, however, there was little doubt. The French ambassador noted: 'It was made public that the gunpowder had been laid by the Lords of Bothwell and Morton who afterwards pretended to be most active in searching out the murderers. They said they were acting for the good of the country and to free the Queen from the misery she had suffered at the hands of Darnley'. Yet a trial in Edinburgh in April acquitted Bothwell. No doubt the presence of three hundred of his men in the courtyard did something to influence the court.

Mary's Third Marriage

Mary might in time have lived down the rumours concerning her involvement, but she damned herself in the eyes of Scotland and threw away her reputation by marrying Bothwell, whom most believed to be her husband's murderer, only three months after Darnley's death. The marriage was a solemn occasion and was conducted according to Protestant practices.

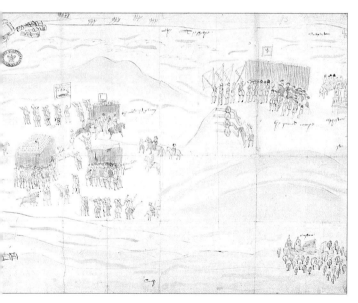

This sketch of the Battle of Carberry hill was done at the time of the battle. In the centre you can see Mary being led away on horseback.

Hostility to Mary grew rapidly, and on 15 June at Carberry Hill outside Edinburgh her opponents confronted the royal army. Bothwell fled, and Mary, as the sketch illustrates, had no choice but to surrender. She was brought to Edinburgh in disgrace. Deserted by friends and husband alike, worn out, travel-weary, ill-clad, her spirit seemed broken.

To make matters worse, she had to suffer the insults thrown at her by the Edinburgh crowd, the same crowd which had cheered her return in 1561. Her capture also coincided with Knox's return to Edinburgh, and he, filled with new energy, demanded in many sermons that Mary, as a murderess and adulteress, be put to death. Knox based his arguments on the same idea that it was lawful for a people to judge and punish an unworthy ruler over which he and Mary had clashed earlier.

Abdication
and Imprisonment

It was decided by Mary's captors that she should be imprisoned and on 16 June, the day after her surrender, she was taken by night across the Firth of Forth and escorted north to Loch Leven. There she was placed in the castle of Sir William Douglas, from which escape was thought impossible. Lochleven Castle was a total contrast to the comforts of Holyrood, lacking furniture, decent bedding, and the spacious apartments to which the Queen was used.

Not that in the eyes of her enemies she was to be Queen for much longer. On 24 July 1567, she agreed under pressure to abdicate in favour of her infant son James, and on 29 July the young prince was crowned James VI at Stirling. Knox was there to preach the sermon. New coins were minted to proclaim the start of the child-king's reign. As he was only an infant, the reins of government were held by his uncle, Lord James Stewart, who had been made Earl of Moray, while the King himself was placed in the care of the staunchly Protestant Earl of Mar. Mary never saw her son again.

Imprisonment at Loch Leven

The young James VI

Loch Leven Castle

It is not surprising that Mary lay in a state of collapse for almost a fortnight. To make matters worse her jailer, Sir William Douglas, placed her in a cramped tower in the corner of the courtyard furthest from the shore, to make signalling for help impossible.

Help came, however, from within the castle walls. Willie Douglas, a youthful member of the Douglas household, was befriended by Mary and agreed to smuggle out correspondence to her friends and to bring their replies. Mary's other ally was George Douglas, Sir William's brother, who fell under her charm. Between them, George and Willie daringly arranged the risky escape. This is what the ambassador from Venice wrote of the event: 'Guard was continually kept in the castle, day and night, except during supper when the gate was locked with a key which lay on the table where the governor took his meals. The Queen planned that a page would place a napkin on top of the key and then remove both without anyone noticing. When he had done this they went to the Queen and told her everything was ready'.

Defeat and Flight   On 2 May 1568 Mary, disguised in a servant's clothes, was nervously led out of her prison into a waiting boat. Every minute held danger of discovery, but their luck held and Mary safely reached the shore where George Douglas was waiting with horses and supplies.

After ten months of imprisonment Mary was free once more. She headed for the heartland of her supporters in the west and was able, on the way, to muster about 5000 men with the intention of occupying the fortress of Dumbarton. While passing Langside to the south of Glasgow, however, her army was attacked and routed on 13 May. Mary panicked. She could have stayed in Scotland and tried to rally her scattered forces, who were to continue to fight for her cause until 1573. She could even have gone to France, where she had lands and money. Instead she fled to England, naively expecting that her cousin, Elizabeth, would welcome her with open arms. On 16 May, wearing borrowed clothes, she crossed the Solway Firth and stepped on to English soil. Her journey was a miserable one. 'I have endured', she wrote, 'injuries, imprisonment, lies, famine, cold, heat and flight to I don't know where, across 92 miles (148kms) of country without stopping or dismounting and then I had to sleep on the ground and drink sour milk, and eat oatmeal without bread'.

Elizabeth I

In her innocence, she thought that she could expect safety and guidance from her cousin. 'Next to God', she wrote to her, 'I trust in you'. All she had done, however, was to put Elizabeth in a very difficult position. After all, Mary had in the past laid claim to Elizabeth's throne, and could still be a source of threats to her.

Should she lock Mary in an English jail for the rest of her life? This proposal was not too sound since it would give English Catholics a rallying-point for their cause in their midst.

Should she send Mary back to Scotland? By doing this Elizabeth might be returning her to certain death, and acknowledging the rights of subjects to rebel against their sovereign.

Should she allow Mary to go to France? To do this might simply give the French and Spanish Catholics the ideal weapon with which to attack England.

Elizabeth was faced with a difficult choice, and while she agonised over a decision Mary was kept under lock and key in Carlisle Castle. Finally, she decided to put Mary on trial for the murder of Darnley. During this trial, held

Imprisonment in England

Above is one of the monograms embroidered by Mary. It contains the intertwined letters of Maria S.

first in York and then at Westminster, the Casket Letters were produced, having been sent by Moray to ensure that Mary was found guilty. The information in them, if true, was damning, but Mary dismissed them as forgeries. Though no firm evidence could be produced, and though Mary was prevented from answering the charges personally in court, she was given what amounted to a life sentence. Thus, for the next nineteen years, Mary was kept in a series of English prisons.

Mary's misery was now complete. She was dethroned, imprisoned in a foreign land, and shut up in the draughty, half-ruined castle of Tutbury. For security reasons she was soon to be moved from castle to castle: Chatsworth, Sheffield, Wingfield Manor, Fotheringhay. She was to spend more of her life a prisoner in England than she ever did in Scotland. To pass her time, Mary would write letters or embroider. One of the mottos she embroidered reads *Virtue flourishes with wounding*. Can we see a hint of Mary's character in this?

Plots...

It is not surprising that Mary was easily drawn into a series of plots which offered her the chance of freedom. The first was organised in 1569 by a group of people who became Mary's supporters for different reasons. Some wanted to get rid of William Cecil, Elizabeth's chief minister; others wanted to ensure that Mary would succeed to the English throne. It was agreed that Mary would divorce Bothwell, now in Denmark, and marry the Duke of Norfolk. To complicate the scheme even more, a group of earls from northern England, where Catholicism was still strong, planned a revolt to overthrow Elizabeth.

Like so many plots designed to help Mary, the scheme came to nothing. Norfolk was imprisoned in the Tower of London and the revolt of the northern earls was crushed. Mary herself was merely moved from one comfortless castle to another.

Mary's circumstances became more difficult in 1570 when the Pope expelled the Protestant Elizabeth from the Catholic Church and encouraged her subjects to rise against her. He stated: 'I take away Elizabeth's false claims to the throne, and English nobles and subjects are

The casket letters

Elizabeth wanted to keep Mary away from London. She decided to hold an enquiry in York in October 1568 to investigate Mary's involvement in Darnley's murder. This would keep Mary in the north. At the enquiry, Mary was shocked by the contents of this silver casket, taken from one of Bothwell's servants. The casket had belonged to Mary, but her enemies said it contained love letters to Bothwell written while Darnley was ill in Glasgow and which implicated her in her husband's death. It is now generally accepted that the letters were crude forgeries: they certainly failed to convince Elizabeth and her advisers, but Mary was still held in prison.

excused of all promises, loyalty or obedience to her. I forbid nobles and subjects to obey her orders or laws'. Elizabeth now had even more reason to believe that the claims of the Catholic Mary might pose a threat to her hold on the English crown.

From Scotland, Knox, who was at the height of his influence though in failing health, urged Elizabeth '... to apply the axe to the root of evil', adding that until '... the Scottish queen was dead, neither her (Elizabeth's) crown nor her life would be in security'. Furthermore, Mary continued to pose a threat to the government in Scotland, for her supporters still waged a civil war against the supporters of her son, James. In January 1570 the Regent Moray had been assassinated, and it was feared that his death, and those of his two immediate successors as regent, would bring chaos to the government and see a revival in Catholic fortunes.

To make matters worse for Mary, two further plots followed fast on the heels of the recently crushed rising of the northern earls. In May 1570 a group of minor Catholic lords drew up a vastly ambitious plan to rescue her from Chatsworth, but Mary herself was distinctly unenthusiastic and refused to become involved. In August, however, a much more damaging conspiracy came to light – the Ridolfi Plot. This was a hare-brained scheme organised by Roberto Ridolfi, an Italian banker who acted as a papal agent. He planned for a Spanish army to invade England, release Norfolk – whom Mary would marry – and establish Mary as Queen of England. The plot was badly organised and soon discovered by Elizabeth's agents. Discovery cost Norfolk his head: Mary was no further forward.

Mary's position seemed even blacker as events in Scotland turned decisively – and finally – against her. Her supporters there had been slowly drifting away and surrendering to the government of King James, but the deaths of Moray, and his colleagues the Earls of Lennox and Mar, held out some hope of recovery. The death, too, in November 1572 of her most outspoken critic, John Knox, must have been welcome news to the dispirited Queen. In October 1572, however, James Douglas, earl of Morton, became Regent. He was one of the men implicated in the murder of Darnley, and a convinced Protestant. Under his leadership the government forces moved swiftly to crush the remnants of Mary's support in Scotland.

In May 1573 two of her staunchest supporters, Sir William Kirkcaldy of Grange and William Maitland of Lethington, were forced to surrender Edinburgh Castle, the last important fortress to be held for Mary. The sketch shows Morton's army, aided by troops sent from England, bombarding the castle into surrender under a continuous artillery barrage. The gallant Kirkcaldy was executed, but Maitland, who had long been ill, died in captivity. The loss of such men effectively ended her cause in Scotland. There was little prospect that her son, King James, would do anything to aid his mother. He had been educated under the supervision of George Buchanan, and had been told that his mother was a wicked woman who had murdered his father to marry her lover, Bothwell. James could hardly be expected to care much about her distress.

... And More Plots

Conspiracies continued to be formed around Mary, though very often she had difficulty in seeing how they

This drawing of the siege of Edinburgh Castle is from Holinshed's Chronicles, *a book written soon after the siege.*

were meant to serve her interests. In 1583 the Throckmorton Plot was discovered. This suggested that Mary had been planning for Spain to launch an invasion of England. Further embarrassment came two years later when it was revealed that a Dr Parry, who had met one of Mary's agents, was planning to assassinate Elizabeth.

These plots were often fanciful, badly planned and easily discovered by Elizabeth's servants. Indeed, some were engineered by the English authorities to trap men whom they suspected of disloyalty. In many cases, Mary had scarcely any knowledge of the plots being hatched in her name, but, with each conspiracy unearthed, Mary's reputation in Elizabeth's eyes was further undermined. It is often difficult to discover how far Mary was involved, but any link with her was enough to cause Elizabeth to wonder how long she could tolerate such a threat to her life.

Unfortunately for Mary she was often caught up in a plot

hoping that it would secure her release, while the real intention of the conspirators was perhaps to discredit one of Elizabeth's ministers, or to further the interests of the Catholic Church, or of France or Spain. It is doubtful if Mary ever had any real intention of overthrowing Elizabeth and restoring Catholicism to England – she had, after all, hardly shown much enthusiasm for plans to reverse the Reformation in Scotland. She was simply more interested in regaining her freedom and returning to the France she loved: Scotland held nothing for her but bitter memories.

The end came for Mary when she became involved in the Babington Plot. Anthony Babington was a wealthy, hot-headed young Catholic who had been a page to Mary's gaoler, Lord Shrewsbury, when she was at Sheffield. He was persuaded to be the leader of a plot to assassinate Elizabeth, bring about a foreign invasion and release Mary. It was arranged that correspondence between Mary and Babington would be hidden in a barrel of ale.

Mary did not realise that this plot was being carefully organised by Walsingham, Elizabeth's secretary of state, a very clever man who had built up a network of spies and agents throughout England. Unknown to Mary all her letters were intercepted and read by Walsingham. Although Mary had secret codes, the wily minister had the key to them. Here is part of a letter written by Mary: "Everything is being prepared and the forces both in and out of England are ready: you must set the six men to work, tell them that when their planning is finished I must be got out of here, order them to have all our forces on the field to receive me while we wait for foreign help".

Arrest

Even when Walsingham had complete details of the plot he wanted to catch Mary red-handed. He arranged for her to be allowed out to watch a hunt while her rooms were searched and her codes confiscated. You can imagine Mary's delight at seeing a group of horsemen galloping towards her across the park as she rode to the hunt. This, she thought, was the end to her captivity. Her joy turned to anger and misery when she realised that, far from being released, she was being arrested for treason.

When Elizabeth was presented with evidence of yet another and more serious plot, she had no alternative but to put Mary on trial for high treason. The sketch shows the layout of the trial at Fotheringhay Castle. Alone in the hostile court, she must have felt fear and despair.

Trial

The verdict was guilty. Only a reprieve from Elizabeth could now save Mary from execution. But no reprieve came, and even King James was not prepared to appeal for the life of the mother whom he could not even remember. On 8 February 1587 Mary Stuart was beheaded in the Great Hall of Fotheringhay Castle. Here is how an eye-witness described the final scene: 'The Queen of Scots sat upon a stool... in her hand a crucifix... and she began, with tears in her voice, to pray loudly in Latin. When she had finished her prayers the executioners asked her to forgive them. She was stripped of her outer garments and blindfolded. Then her two ladies left her and she knelt down upon the cushion

Execution

Mary's execution

most resolutely, without any sign of fear of death, and groping for the block, she laid down her head, putting her chin over the block with both hands. Then she cried out, with her hands outstretched "Into your hands, O Lord" three or four times. She endured two strokes of the executioner's axe and made a very small noise or none at all and so the executioner cut off her head, except for a small piece of gristle. Then he held up her head to the view of all the assembly and shouted, "God save the Queen!" Then the Dean said with a loud voice, "So perish all the Queen's enemies!" Then one of the executioner's spied the Queen of Scots' little dog which was unwilling to leave her corpse.'

From Fotheringhay, Mary's body was taken for burial to Peterborough Cathedral. It remained there until 1612 when her son, who had not lifted a finger to aid her in her captivity or to appeal to Elizabeth to allow her to live in 1587, had her remains transferred to the magnificent tomb in Westminster Abbey.

This is a model of Mary's tomb in Westminster Abbey

The story of Mary Stuart is one which still arouses strong emotions nowadays. To many she is a tragic heroine, overwhelmed then destroyed by forces and events outwith her control, while to others she was a foolish woman and a failure who was eventually to fall victim to her own ambitions.

For all her failures and disappointments, however, Mary ultimately had one triumph. In 1603 the childless Elizabeth of England died and Mary's son, King James VI, succeeded to the throne which his mother had claimed since 1558. While Elizabeth's family died with her, Mary's continued and all Britain's rulers since 1603 have been descended from her, giving truth to the words which she embroidered during her long captivity: "In my end is my Beginning".

Bibliography

David Breeze, *A Queen's Progress* (HMSO, 1987). [This is mainly a guide to the many sites and monuments associated with Mary which are in the care of Historic Scotland.]

Patrick Collinson, *The English Captivity of Mary Queen of Scots*, (Sheffield History Pamphlets, University of Sheffield, 1987). [This contains many useful documents concerning Mary's imprisonment in England.]

Ian B. Cowan, *Mary Queen of Scots* (Edinburgh, 1987).

Antonia Fraser, *Mary Queen of Scots* (London, 1994). [This is the most detailed modern biography of the queen.]

Rosalind Marshall, *Queen of Scots* (HMSO, 1987).

Margaret H. B. Sanderson, *Mary Stewart's People* (Edinburgh, 1987). [A series of essays about some of Mary's subjects, ranging from a tailor to noblemen.]

Jenny Wormald, *Court, Kirk and Community. Scotland 1470-1625* (London, 1981). [Provides a broad overview of the main developments through the sixteenth century in Scotland and sets Mary and Knox into their proper perspective.]

Jenny Wormald, *Mary Queen of Scots: a Study in Failure* (London, 1988)

Acknowledgements

The publishers are grateful to the following organisations and individuals for permission to reproduce illustrations.

The front cover shows a detail of a posthumous portrait of Mary Queen of Scots from Falkland Palace, reproduced by permission of the National Trust for Scotland: *pages 5, 34, 38* Historic Scotland: *page 6, 39* by courtesy of the National Portrait Gallery, London: *pages 7, 15, 26, 31, 37, 45, 46, 47* Scottish National Portrait Gallery: *pages 8, 10, 11, 13, 17* Mansell Collection: *pages 9, 16 top, 21, 33* National Gallery of Scotland: *page 12* Marischal Museum, the University of Aberdeen: *pages 14, 18, 27* by permission of the Trustees of the National Library of Scotland: *page 19, 20, 22* Edinburgh Public Libraries: *page 24* the Bridgeman Art Library and Towneley Hall Art Gallery and Museum, Burnley: *page 25* National Museums of Scotland: *pages 35, 36* Public Record Office: *page 40* Victoria and Albert Museum, London: *page 41* His Grace the Duke of Hamilton and the Lennoxlove Trust. Every effort has been made to trace holders of copyright, and we apologise to any whom it has proved impossible to contact.